Martha and Mary

Copyright © 1993 by Hunt & Thorpe
Text © Rhona Pipe
Illustrations © Annabel Spenceley
Originally published by Hunt and Thorpe 1993
Reissued in 1997
ISBN 1-85608-326-8

The CIP catalogue record for this book is available from the British Library.

Hunt & Thorpe is a name used under licence
by Paternoster Publishing, P.O. Box 300,
Kingstown Broadway, Carlisle, CA3 OQS

Printed in Malaysia

Martha and Mary

Rhona Pipe

Illustrated by
Jenny Press

paternoster
publishing

HUNT&
THORPE

No one was moving
in the streets of the village
on the hillside.
A dog was sleeping in the sun.
The women were sewing or cooking
in the shade by their houses.

All of a sudden
there was a noise.

'Did you hear that?'
Mary said to her sister Martha.
'I'm sure there was a noise.
I'm going to find out.'

'Come quick,' Mary said.
'It's Jesus and his friends —
a crowd of them.
Let's invite them for a meal.
Come on! You ask him.
You're the eldest.'

'Jesus!' Martha said.
'Why didn't you tell us you
were coming?
It's great to see you again.
Will you come for a meal — er —
all of you?'

Martha was thrilled,
but she was also upset.

There was so much to do.
First she had to buy more food,
and wash it
and cook it.
And bake bread.
And put it all out nicely.
And pour out drinks.

No. First she had to go to the well
for more water
for Jesus and his friends to wash.
And find lots of towels
from somewhere.

But first she had to borrow
more cups and plates and . . .
Martha needed help.
Where was Mary?

Mary was with Jesus, of course.
She was sitting on the ground
with the others.
All Mary wanted to do
was listen to Jesus.

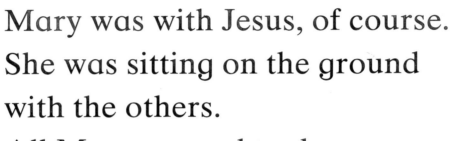

Martha felt like crying.
She said, 'Jesus.
Don't you care about me?
I've got all this work to do.
All by myself.
It's not fair.
Tell Mary she's got to help.'

Jesus looked at Martha and smiled.
'Oh, Martha,' he said.
'You're too fussed up.
You put the wrong things first.
Only one thing is really important.
And Mary's got it right.'

What do you think Martha did then?